PAC-MAN FEVER

The Story Behind the Unlikely '80's Hit That Defined a Worldwide Craze

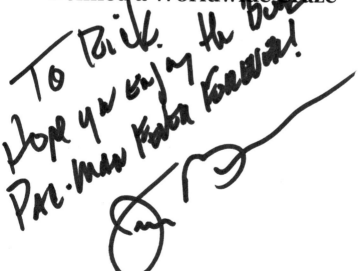

To Talia, With Love,

Hope you enjoy reading!

Best wishes, Karen Romano Young

PAC-MAN FEVER

The Story Behind
the Unlikely '80's Hit That
Defined a Worldwide Craze

Jerry Buckner
Mike Stewart
Editor Terrie M Buckner, EdD

DME PUBLISHING
NASHVILLE, TENNESSEE

Copyright © 2020 by Jerry Buckner, Mike Stewart & Digital Music eBooks Publishing

All rights reserved. Brief passages of this book may be used in reviews but, except as allowed by United States copyright law, no part of this book may be reproduced or transmitted in any form or by any means, electronic, mechanical, magnetic, photographic including photocopying, recording or by any information storage and retrieval system without prior written permission of the publisher. No patent liability is assumed with respect to the use of the information contained herein and the publisher and author assume no responsibility for errors, inaccuracies, omissions, or inconsistencies.

ISBN: 978-0-943941-11-0

Published by:
DME | Digital Music eBooks
Nashville, Tennessee
https://digitalmusicebooks.com/

Table of Contents

Introduction vii
1. How It Started 1
2. The Genesis Of Pac-Man Fever 4
3. Taking Matters Into Their Own Hands & Breaking Through on Radio 7
4. Making the Album 10
5. Duel With .38 Special 13
6. How The State of Florida Saved Pac-Man Fever 15
7. The Promotional Tour 17
8. Crazy Fame 23
9. 80's Pop Culture Icons 27
10. Wreck-It Ralph Theme Song 34
11. Downloads & Multimedia Content 36
12. Pac-Man Fever Sheet Music & Lyrics 39
13. Free Gift 43

Introduction

If you're a child of the early 1980s it is likely that you were consumed by the ubiquitous Pac-Man video games that seemed to be everywhere at the time. The game not only spawned a worldwide craze but a million-selling gold record for the Buckner & Garcia duo called "Pac-Man Fever".

In so many ways, "Pac-Man Fever" became the soundtrack for an era and the unofficial theme song of one of the most popular video games in history. This book captures the story of that song and history that led it to be the unlikely smash hit of 1982.

This eBook is specifically designed for fans of the song, the Pac-Man game and the 1980s. The stories in the book were derived primarily from interviews and conversations with Jerry Buckner and some of the stories appear in third person narrative. Not only will you read about the history of the music but we've included exclusive and extended downloadable tracks of the song (including a karaoke version) as well sheet music. Also included are never before seen behind the scenes photos and links to videos and other exclusive multimedia content. Enjoy!!!

1

How It Started

To really understand how "Pac-Man Fever" came about, you'd have to go back several years prior to it becoming a hit to see what Jerry Buckner and Gary Garcia were into at the time. They had both been playing in bands since high school in Akron, Ohio, and they eventually ended up in Atlanta, Georgia together. They began writing jingles and creating commercials there, in addition to playing in their band at night, in order to make a living. They were pop songwriters who always had multiple projects going, and they were doing everything they could to make deals and push songs.

Jokingly, Jerry made the comment one day, "Why don't we just do a song with a beat? Maybe they'll like that. You know, something just stupidly repetitive." So, they dreamed up a fictional character, which they named Animal Jack, and they recorded

a record. "It was horrible, really, but it was meant to be a joke. A guy was screaming, 'Gotta hear the beat...' about halfway through, and then this would stop before kicking back in again." Jerry states, "It was definitely a novelty song," but they ended up selling it to Laurie Records, which was a major label at the time.

The band ended up selling their single to three different labels, and this was the first time they had ventured into the world of producing novelty records. A few years after that, they produced another record of a similar style, and it was called "Merry Christmas in the NFL." The artist for this song was Bob Carr. He worked in radio, and he had a voice that sounded southern, so they thought he would be a good candidate for singing the song.

That song went through the Buie/Geller group, with Arnie Geller and Buddy Buie. They had a production company in Atlanta, which had a number of acts, including the Atlanta Rhythm Section and Alicia Bridges of "I Love the Nightlife" fame. They managed to get a deal for the song and had it released. It didn't make it very high on the charts, but it was the first charted song Jerry and Gary had. They were excited for the success, but they turned back around and started making jingles again because the records weren't really making them much money. They did get a little bit of recognition, but they were still struggling to attain success.

2

The Genesis of Pac-Man Fever

Gary and Jerry went to eat dinner one night at a restaurant named Shillings on the Square in Marietta, Georgia, a city northwest of Atlanta. It was a very popular restaurant at the time, and it's still in operation today.

When Gary and Jerry arrived, they noticed that a table in the middle of the place had a tabletop that was a game, and it turned out to be a Pac-Man machine. They decided to play it, and they were instantly hooked, just like everyone else there that day. This caused them to start spending more time at the restaurant while they were working on various projects going on at a studio nearby.

They saw how the Pac-Man craze was really starting to catch on. That's when they decided to record a song about the game that they thought might help their jingle business. So, Jerry went home and played around on the piano a bit, and it wasn't long before he had an idea for the chorus. He says that he wrote out a couple of verses, and then he took what he had to Gary. After that, Gary added his lyrical genius, and when they thought they had something, they went to Buie/Geller and played the song for them. They really liked it, and they were aware of the game too.

Buie/Geller told them that they could go ahead and cut the song in their studio. That's what they started to do, but it wasn't long before they determined that they weren't happy with the lyrics. Gary rewrote the lyrics, and he's responsible for the infamous line, "I got a pocket full of quarters, and I'm headed to the arcade." That summed up the time period so well. In addition to Pac-Man, there were all kinds of games you could play in an arcade, such as Asteroids,

Centipede and others. "People were just pouring quarters into these games, and so that line was just genius. It really captured what was going on at the time."

The band went into the studio and recorded "Pac-Man Fever". Everyone liked it, and they thought it sounded like a hit, so Arnie went to New York and shopped the song around to the major labels to see if anyone would take it on.

They were welcomed to a chorus of crickets.

Labels didn't understand the song, and they didn't understand Pac-Man. It's hard to believe this now, considering how much Pac-Man has become a part of our culture.

Back then, it was new, and they just didn't know what it was. Not only that, but they received letters from the labels where the song had been shopped that commented they didn't think it was a hit, period.

Suffice to say, they were very disappointed.

3

Taking Matters Into Their Own Hands & Breaking Through on Radio

Fortunately, Buie/Geller had a label of their own, so they went ahead and put it out. This was in the fall of 1981. It was released locally in October. They got a local radio station to play it. Many people mistakenly think morning show personality Gary McKee played it for the first time, but he didn't. A DJ named Jim Morrison sitting in for a vacationing McKee actually played it first.

When Jim played it, he had a tremendous response. He had so many requests that he played it again within the same hour, which was something they just didn't do in radio at the time.

On the air, he actually said, "Arnie, you've got a smash record. You've got to get moving on this."

Jerry said, "It was just crazy to have that happen on the air like that, live." By the end of the week records were flying out the door.

Jerry and Gary were kind of in limbo because no one major label had bought it yet, and they were a little depressed because they didn't know what was going to happen.

Jerry recalls being at a sandwich shop when they decided to go to the studio office to check in as there were no cell phones back then. When they arrived, Arnie was on his balcony, which overlooked the parking lot, shouting, "Get in here! Get in here!"

They hurried in, and Arnie informed them that CBS/Columbia Records was on the phone and wanted the record. CBS' VP Mickey Eichner's said, "We've got to have this thing." He flew down the next day and they signed a deal right then, and everyone was feeling pretty good about all of it.

4

Making the Album

CBS told Jerry and Gary that they needed an album. So, they decided to start working on the album, and since they were writers, they already had a lot of pop songs made (that they had written). They created two songs for the album, and then Mickey flew down to see what they were up to. He stopped them right in their tracks and said, "No, no, no! We want it to be all game songs."

This took the team aback. "All game songs?

That's going to put us in just one niche," they replied.

Still, CBS was firm on their stance. The team didn't want to waste the songs they already had completed because a lot of money had already been spent on them.

Gary created new lyrics to the melodies, and they redid the songs so that they were game songs. This

was a struggle because there were a lot of games coming out at the time, but they didn't really know much about them. Plus, they weren't given a lot of time to work on them.

Gary and Jerry went out to different arcades to play games and get some ideas. They took the time to figure out which games were the most popular too. So they would hang out and talk to the people who were playing the games.

After taking all of this in, they would go back to the studio and work on more songs. They did that for each of the songs over the next week, and they recall it being very stressful and kind of tough to do.

They were excited, though, and happy to be doing it. Everything was okay. Afterwards, they felt like the album turned out pretty well, considering all they had to do in a short amount of time. They didn't get much sleep, and they worked hard on it every day. At that point in the fall season, the record companies were in a little bit of a lull to get them up and press them, but they put it out nationally.

5

Duel with .38 Special

While Jerry and Gary were recording their album during the day, 38 Special was recording a new album of theirs at night. Of course, Jerry and Gary thought 38 Special was a great band, but the engineer that was working with them there, at the studio, kept going on and on about how great 38 Special's music was, and he was giving the "Pac-Man Fever" team a hard time. After a while, they just got tired of hearing it.

Greg was the name of this engineer, and, eventually, Jerry made a comment to him about it. He said, "Hey, it's just a bunch of guitars and shit." The team had a big laugh about that, but Greg relayed that story to the 38 Special band members when they came in the next time. Well, the 38 Special band members didn't think it was so funny, and somehow, Gary got blamed for the line instead of Jerry. So, the other band members drew a picture of Gary, making him look like a fat Neanderthal. It had a belt with Pac-Man on it, and it just made him look really bad.

The picture was stuck up over the door, and when Gary saw it, he wasn't very happy about it at all. Well, a week or so later, Gary came in with a mockup of an album cover, and he had commissioned an artist to make it look real. It said "38 Special" up at the top, and then, under the name, there was a picture of a pile of dog excrement with little lines coming up from it, indicating the smell. There were flies drawn around the pile too. There was also a list of songs written on it, and the songs were titled things like, "Guitars & Shit" and "Two Guitars & a Pile of Shit."

Jerry still laughs about how hilarious this was to this day. Gary stuck the album cover he had made on the wall over the door. Apparently, when the 38 Special band members came in later that night, they really did not like that. They didn't have any sense of humor about it at all; in fact, one of the band members threatened to beat Gary up over it.

Jerry backs up his friend when he tells this story, saying, "Gary isn't anyone you'd want to make mad. He could definitely take care of himself." Anyway, that's just a humorous story about something that was going on at the time. The album cover mockup that Gary had made still exists, but apparently, Greg won't hand it back over to Gary and Jerry.

6

How the State of Florida Saved Pac-Man Fever

Nothing really happened at first. Nothing seemed to be going on, but then, they got into the Christmas holidays. In "The Business", at least in those days, they would go into something that they would call "a freeze" in which the charts would freeze for two weeks for Christmas and New Year's Day. Nothing would happen, and you were completely out of the loop.

Over the holidays that year, Gary and Jerry were thinking optimistically, but they were wondering what was going on because they had no news. So, they held a meeting with everyone at the office right after New Year's to see what was going on, and it was depressing. Buddy Buie announced to them that he was afraid the record was dead; that there just wasn't anything going on with the song.

That was not accurate because, shortly after, they discovered that the song was getting heavy play in Florida, and then they found out they were getting some play in Michigan.

It turned out to be that over the Christmas holidays, a lot of the people from the Northern United States, who went to Florida for the holidays, had heard the song when on vacation in the Sunshine State. These people heard it and loved it. So, when they got back to Detroit, Cleveland, New York, and all of these major cities, they started requesting it from the local radio stations. This grass roots popularity got the record a lot of attention.

Things started to really pick up, and WAGA Channel 5 in Atlanta, came to the studio to interview Jerry and Gary. That story went national including running on *Entertainment Tonight* (and) that's what made things truly take off.

7

The Promotional Tour

Gary and Jerry found out that they were going to have to go to California to do some TV shows and promote the song. They were excited about that, and Gary had an idea to do something crazy to make them more memorable since they were doing these TV shows.

Jerry asked him, "Well, how crazy do you want to get?"

And, Gary just said, "Oh, you know, just something kind of wild, but let's not tell each other, and we'll surprise each other when we get out to California."

Jerry agreed to the idea. He had always been a Groucho Marx fan, and then there was also a character he liked that used to be on TV in Cleveland, Ohio, named Ghoulardi. He was a very popular late-night movie host back in the '60s who used to wear a crazy wig and lab coat with buttons pinned all over it. So,

Jerry decided to act out a character that was a combo of Groucho and Ghoulardi.

They got to California, and they went to do the first show, which was *Solid Gold*. It was a big show at the time. When they got to the studio, Jerry got one dressing room and Gary got another. Jerry started to get into character, putting a lab coat on and painting a mustache onto his face. He also added a pair of white garden gloves to the mix. They both stepped out of the dressing room, but Gary looked like he always did, so Jerry said, "Hey man, you got to get ready."

To which Gary replied, "Well, I am ready."

Confused, Jerry asked, "What do you mean? You said we should dress crazy."

Gary said, "Yeah, I said we should do something different." Well, he had taken a little Pac Man about the size of a dime and pasted it on his sunglasses. It was on the edge of one of the lenses, and he had a little hat on that said, "Garcia." That was it. That's what he considered crazy.

As soon as Jerry figured out what was going on, they got called onstage. So, they went out and made their appearance.

Marilyn McCoo was one of the hosts of the show. She's a very beautiful woman, and she's a great singer. She's been very successful and was with The 5th Dimension. As they walked up on stage, Marilyn asked, "Who are you supposed to be?" Jerry felt like an idiot, but there was no time to change. They did the show, and Jerry said it was horrible. To this day, he doesn't like to watch that clip. To make matters worse, when the show aired in Atlanta a week or two later, Jerry got a phone call from his mom. She was very upset because all her friends tuned in to watch. Regardless, that was the experience he had when he appeared on *Solid Gold*.

Jerry also notes that on that show they had edited the song some. In the middle of the song, Gary's hat had fallen off. Well, they didn't include the part where his hat fell off. So, he's singing and playing with his hat on in the beginning, and then, all of a sudden, he's singing and playing without a hat. Jerry chuckles as he recalls all of this and just says, "Yeah, that's the *Solid Gold* story."

(Check out the link to this hilarious clip in Chapter 11 Downloads & Multimedia Content)

At one point, they had all of the major networks calling, and when you picked up the phone, you didn't know who it was going to be. It could have been *American Bandstand*, CBS, ABC, or even *The TODAY Show* or *Good Morning America*. It was such a big story, and these men were getting interviews from everyone.

MTV was fairly new at the time, and they featured the song throughout the day. Here Dick Clark interviews Jerry and Gary on American Bandstand.

They also appeared on Nickelodeon. They had a sort of talk show for teenagers at the time in which guests would talk and the audience would ask questions. Well, they were going to have an episode about video games because it was a big, hot topic in those days. The filming actually took place at the Ed Sullivan Theater. Jerry thought that was really cool because that's where the Beatles had appeared.

Jerry remembers standing in the elevator, and they only had one in the building. "It was so slow and small that it took forever," he says, "and I had to use the restroom, and I didn't know what to do because we had to be on stage pretty quickly. So, I asked one of the stagehands if there was a bathroom around. 'Well, you can go around here and use the sink. If it was good enough for John Lennon, it should be good enough for you.'"

Afterwards, Gary and Jerry were in the green room with everyone who was going to be on the show. There were various TV show actors and some reps from video game companies. Also, there were some women there who had started some sort of anti-game movement, and, according to Jerry, they were really into it because they were finally getting some press for their cause. Well, everyone was stuck in there closely together, and, of course, the anti-gamers and the people who were for the games eventually got into an argument. It got ugly while they were waiting for the show to start.

Gary and Jerry were sitting next to one of the women who were rallying against the games, and Jerry said that he was hoping that they wouldn't find out who they were because, essentially, they were poster boys for video games.

Well, sure enough, the woman they were sitting beside turned around and asked, "Aren't you the guys who did the 'Pac-Man Fever' record?" Jerry very quietly and hesitantly admitted that they were, and then what happened next took him by total surprise. She leaned over and asked him for an autograph because her daughter loved that record. Right after that, she walked out on stage and started running down video games, which Jerry found amusing.

A lot of times, Jerry and Gary would be asked to appear at a local arcade and the arcade owners always had the same idea, which was to have kids play against them. Since the kids would play these games all day long, they were always a lot better at the games, and Jerry and Gary would always get beat. They thought it was kind of funny, though, that every one of those venue owners thought that it was an original idea.

8

Crazy Fame

One day, they got word that Freddy Cannon had called their manager because he wanted to meet them. He had a bunch of hits in the late '50s and early '60s. "Palisades Park" and "Tallahassee Lassie" were a couple of the songs he was famous for. It was a big deal for Jerry and Gary to be able to meet him because they had grown up listening to his records.

Freddy was on a show with Frankie Avalon, and they were appearing at the Fox Theatre in Atlanta, so he invited Gary and Jerry to come down there. Their wives were with them at this performance. Beatles Story was hanging out with them that night as well. Tommy was from Atlanta, and he had produced several hits back in his day too. In fact, prior to breaking out worldwide the Beatles opened for Tommy on his British tour.

The group watched the show at the Fox Theatre, and they all went backstage after the show to meet

Freddy. Freddy kept going on and on about "Pac-Man Fever" and how he could have had a hit if he had recorded the song.

When word gets around that you have a hit record, things get crazy. Jerry recalls one morning, he had just woken up and he heard knocking on the door. He went down to answer it, with his hair still all messed up, and there were some neighbors of his at the door who had some other people with them. They told Jerry that the strangers were friends from Michigan who wanted to meet him. So, that's one example of the kind of thing that would go on.

Another time, Jerry went to one of his son's Little League baseball games, and people in the crowd found out that the creator of "Pac-Man Fever" was there. All these kids started approaching him, but it reached a point where it was disruptive because everyone was there to watch the game. So he told the kids to meet him behind the backstops and he would sign autographs. He didn't mind doing that, but the whole scenario was a little embarrassing. Similarly, one time they were out trying to buy a Christmas tree and kids started yelling out the window at him, which was kind of embarrassing too.

Once, his son was playing football and they heard the cheerleaders were cheering to "Pac-Man Fever".

Jerry also heard on TV that people were singing "Pac-Man Fever" at a Green Bay Packers game, which he and Gary thought was cool. During this time period, a story appeared in the paper about Imelda Marcos and her husband, and they stated that "Pac-Man Fever" was her favorite song. Jerry said that was one of the stranger things that had ever happened pertaining to the song.

Jerry also remembers someone starting a college course about "Pac-Man Fever" and video games. He couldn't recall all of the details, but he still can't imagine who would sign up for something like that. In any case, that added to the craziness that went on regarding the song. Something that also happened during the craze for the song was a gold record party that was held for them. Buie/Geller rented the place where it was held, and a lot of press attended. The record was just so huge, and it was taking the country by storm.

Arnie Geller was acting as their manager, and during the party, he took them into the bathroom to talk. Arnie, Jerry, and Gary were all standing in this little space in the bathroom. Arnie began by congratulating them, and then he pulled out two envelopes, and told them, "This is just a little taste of what's coming." They both opened their envelopes and inside of each was a check for $60,000! Jerry and Gary were shocked. After all, a couple of weeks before that, they were taking soda bottles back for the refund money so that they could put get to the studio. The whole situation was just mind-boggling to them.

9

80s Pop Culture Icons

The team didn't get to play many live performances. They had been offered some touring at amusement parks and places like that, but they didn't feel like doing much of that. So they didn't do many live shows. They did do one at a venue called The Moon Shadow, and Jerry remembers this because it was a special night.

Entertainment Tonight came there to interview them because "E.T. I Love You" was their third single, and they wanted to do a story about that.

The craze over "Pac-Man Fever" has continued over the years, and its revival is very big right now.

Jerry says it's amazing to be attached to that time period and the song. Sometimes he can't believe, how many people remember and how the song just carries on and on. "We've become 80s pop culture icons. There are just so many cool things that continue to happen to Gary and Jerry, like a few years ago, "Pac-Man Fever" was played at the Rose Bowl mention. It has also been played on several television shows, including *The Simpsons, South Park, Family Guy, The Tonight Show,* and *TODAY.* It just turns up all over the place.

One of the neatest things that Jerry has ever gotten to do, concerning "Pac-Man Fever" was be a part of the 35th Anniversary of Pac-Man. There was an event held in Chicago, and he got to meet Toru Iwatani, who is the creator of Pac-Man. Here Jerry and Mike Stewart playing at that event.

Toru spoke very little English, and there was a film crew from Japan with him. It was a big occasion, and a lot of people were in attendance, but Jerry got to visit with Toru for a little while and shake hands with him. He said that Toru even leaned over and sung a little of "Pac-Man Fever" into his ear, which was incredible!

Jerry says that he has a poster that Toru drew one of the Pac-Man characters on and then signed. He says that he really doesn't know what it says because it's in Japanese, but he'd love to know. Here's the poster... Anyone know what Toru wrote?

Pac-Man Fever

1982

PAC MAN
The arcade game—the name comes from Japanese slang for "chomp"—quickly eats up $1 billion in quarters in its first year, and even inspires a Top 10 novelty hit, "Pac Man Fever."

and partner A.E. Hotchner wrote in their book *Newman's Own*. "Fortunately, we don't know any of them"

208 / Pritikin diet
The Pritikin Program for Diet and Exercise— which advocates straight-from-nature foods like fruits, vegetables, beans and brown rice— sells 10 million copies

211 / *Family Ties*,
a sitcom about '60s liberals trying to raise their young Republican offspring, makes Michael J. Fox a star

212 / Gravity boots
Special footwear that allows users to hang upside down—the better to improve posture and blood flow to the brain, allegedly—are a (very brief) trend

213 / Deely Bobbers
Goofy, alien-looking antennae, with little balls on the end, are selling at the rate of 10,000 a day

214 / "I'm Larry. This is my brother Darryl. This is my other brother Darryl"
Newhart, starring, conveniently, Bob Newhart as a Vermont innkeeper surrounded by quirky locals, premieres and will run for eight years. In an inspired finale, he wakes up in bed, looks over and sees Suzanne Pleshette, his wife from his earlier *The Bob Newhart Show*. "Honey," he says, "you won't believe the dream I just had"

215 / Falklands War
erupts. Argentina stakes a military claim to South Atlantic islands that Great Britain has claimed for 150 years.

209
▶ JANE FONDA'S WORKOUT
works out spectacularly for Jane Fonda, selling 17 million copies and helping to popularize the VCR

In 2011, Jerry and Gary were part of a special issue of *People Magazine*. They featured some of the top pop culture events over the last 50 years. "Pac-Man Fever" was featured as one of them.

Some of the musicians who helped with the song include Ginny Whitaker who was on drums. She had played with Country Joe and the Fish. She was a top-notch drummer. Chris Bowman played lead and rhythm guitar. He has his own music school now.

Rick Hinkle also contributed his musical talents to the song. He played some of the guitar parts on "Pac-Man Fever" and a few of the other tracks that Jerry and Gary produced. Mike Stewart also contributed to "Pac-Man Fever". He's also known for playing the Moog synthesizer on "Mousetrap" and "Going Berserk". He is still very active and successful to this day. Mike is one of Jerry and Gary's closest friends.

Steve Carlisle and Sharron Scott provided the background vocals. Sharron is a terrific vocalist who resides in the Atlanta area. David "Cozy" Cole played syndrum on "Pac-Man Fever". He has a band called Band X, which is one of the top "party bands" in the country.

That's the crew that they had for that particular song, and, of course, there were some different people involved in creating the other tracks on the album. Larry McDonald came in to play bass, but overall it was primarily the same people working together to produce the album. These are all tremendous musicians, and they made the songs on the album come alive.

Today many people ask Jerry about "Jason's Space Gun" that is listed in the credits on the album cover. His 5-year old, son Jason had a space gun that made a lot of different noises that were supposed to be from outer space. In the 1980s they had no way to create those noises in the studio, so they used Jason's Space Gun to create some of the sound effects on the album.

FRONT RUNNERS

A pair of Pac-Man addicts polish off a golden disc of their own and it's eating its way up the music charts

Look out Pac-Man and Ms. Pac-Man, another disc's in hot pursuit, gobbling up a fortune in quarters. This musical critter, *Pac-Man Fever* (Columbia, $7.98), made a beeline to the record charts. When composers Jerry Buckner and Gary Garcia saw their "Pac-Man" single reaching the high-mercury zones of the music world, they turned away from the arcades and went back to their studio. Before a single LP reached a record store, the album had already gone gold—tallied a half-million in sales just from orders based on feverish anticipation.

Buckner and Garcia begin their energized pop ditty with computer bleeps, music to the ears of a Pac-Man fan. Garcia's ode strikes a familiar chord with game addicts: "I've got a pocketful of quarters and I'm headed to the arcade." The chorus, fired by Buckner's keyboards, sums it up: "I've got Pac-Man Fever. It's driving me crazy."

The veteran songwriters, both from Atlanta, immortalize other video games—Mousetrap, the Invader, Centipede—on their new album. "We concentrate on making songs that are enjoyable, exciting and different," says Buckner. "It's an antidote to the world's misery." Soon Buckner and Garcia will incorporate their music into arcade games, cartoons and movies. Exlaims Garcia: "This is a cultural phenomenon, and we've become national heroes."

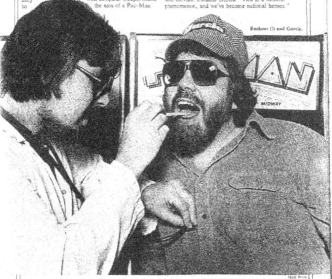

Buckner (l) and Garcia.

10

Wreck-It Ralph Theme Song

It's amazing how an association with a pop-culture era can have such longevity. Case in point, when Disney was making the *Wreck-It Ralph* movie a very talented songwriter by the name of Jamie Houston had written the theme song for the movie called "Wreck It, Wreck-It Ralph." John C. Reilly, who voiced Ralph in the movie, was slated to sing the song, but ultimately it was decided that someone else should sing it.

That's when Disney's senior V.P. of music, Tom MacDougall, remembered "Pac-Man Fever" and immediately decided that it'd be cool to have Buckner & Garcia sing the song. Unfortunately, Gary had died the year before and the remaining band members were given just two weeks to produce it, but they successfully delivered the theme song of the movie,

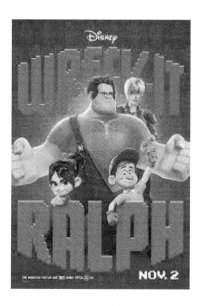

"Wreck it, Wreck Ralph" which appears both in the movie and the soundtrack.

Fortunately, the movie met with both popular and critical success and Jerry and the band were delighted that the movie was nominated for an Academy Award for Best Animated Feature.

11

Downloads & Multimedia Content

You've heard the story of "Pac-Man Fever" now it's time to dig into the music and experience some of the behind-the-scenes video content. To download the music simply navigate to the links below and save them to your music folder. Enjoy!

Songs on the *Pac-Man Fever* album:

Navigate to these links...
Pac-Man Fever -
http://hyperurl.co/r9bdtm

Froggy's Lament
http://hyperurl.co/wn08jc

Ode to a Centipede
http://hyperurl.co/q09ldi

Do the Donkey Kong
http://hyperurl.co/fgum1f

Hyperspace
http://hyperurl.co/vemujn

The Defender
http://hyperurl.co/3f16oh

Mousetrap
http://hyperurl.co/vg3lfv

Goin' Berzerk
http://hyperurl.co/1zkjyr

Country version of Pac-Man Fever
http://hyperurl.co/2ztybj

Karaoke Version
http://hyperurl.co/7lnwhv

Videos

One of only two occasions when "Pac-Man Fever" was played live. It was the guitar player Chris Bowman's wedding... Enjoy!
http://hyperurl.co/xeiz70

Solid Gold - Pac-Man Fever (Note: This is the clip that Jerry a/k/a Groucho is still embarrassed about. And check out when Gary loses his hat!)
http://hyperurl.co/ufew22

American Bandstand – Pac-Man Fever (Note: Check out the interview with Dick Clark after the performance)
http://hyperurl.co/p34nap

Pac-Man Fever (Eat 'Em Up) feat. Jace Hall
http://hyperurl.co/xeebzs

Family Guy Pac-Man Fever
http://hyperurl.co/llka9j

South Park Pac-Man Fever
http://hyperurl.co/2jasnr

The Simpsons Pac-Man Fever
http://hyperurl.co/w6i7pc

12

Pac-Man Fever Sheet Music & Lyrics

Download a PDF of the sheet music of the song here…
http://hyperurl.co/oufob1

* * *

I got a pocketful of quarters
And I'm headed to the arcade
I don't have a lot of money
But I'm bringing everything I made

I got a callus on my finger
And my shoulder's hurtin', too
I'm gonna eat 'em all up
Just as soon as they turn blue

'Cause I got Pac Man Fever (Pac Man Fever)
It's drivin' me crazy (Drivin' me crazy)

I got Pac-Man Fever (Pac-Man Fever)
I'm goin' outta my mind (Goin' outta my mind)
I got Pac-Man Fever (Pac-Man Fever)
I'm goin' outta my mind (Goin' outta my mind)

[musical interlude - 4 measures]

I've got all the patterns down
Up until the ninth key
I've got Speedy on my tail
And I know it's either him or me

So I'm heading out the back door
And in the other side
I'm gonna eat the cherries up
And take em' all for a ride

I got Pac-Man Fever (Pac-Man Fever)
It's drivin' me crazy (Drivin' me crazy)
I got Pac-Man Fever (Pac-Man Fever)
I'm goin' outta my mind (Goin' outta my mind)
I got Pac-Man Fever (Pac-Man Fever)
I'm goin' outta my mind (Goin' outta my mind)

[musical interlude - 2 measures]

I'm gonna fake to the left
Then move to the right
'Cause Pokey's too slow

And Blinky'soutta sight

[instrumental break - 16 measures]

Now I've got them on the run
And I'm lookin' for the high score.
So it's once around the block
Then I slide back out the side door.

Uhh!!

I'm really cookin' now
Eatin' everything in sight
All my monies gone
So I'll be back tomorrow night

'Cause I got Pac-Man Fever (Pac-Man Fever)
It's drivin' me crazy (Drivin' me crazy)
I got Pac-Man Fever (Pac-Man Fever)
I'm goin' outta my mind (Goin' outta my mind)
I got Pac-Man Fever (Pac-Man Fever)
Drivin' me
Drivin' me
Drivin' me crazy
Pac-Man Fever (Pac-Man Fever)
I'm goin' outta my mind (Goin' outta my mind)
Pac-Man Fever (Pac-Man Fever)
It's drivin' me crazy (Drivin' me crazy)

I got Pac-Man Fever (Pac-Man Fever)
I'm goin' outta my mind (Goin' outta my mind)
P-P-P-P-Pac-Man Fever (Pac-Man Fever)
[fade out]

© 1982 Jerry Buckner & Gary Garcia / BGO Music Inc.

13

Free Gift

Jerry and the band thank you so much for being a fan. They truly appreciate you and as a token of that appreciation they are giving you free access to the "Pac-Man Fever" Vault. If you liked this book you'll love all the goodies in the vault including never before released music and more "Pac-Man Fever" trivia.

To get your gift all you got to do is navigate to this link and register… it's 100% FREE !

https://tinyurl.com/pacmanfevervault